TO

_____

FROM

_____

DATE

_____

GOD'S GOT A PERFECT RECORD
for keeping promises.

He hears your every prayer today and vows to give you hope that you can believe in. If you are trying to overcome fear, He promises to give you His strength. If you are hurting, He will give comfort and fill you with peace. He promises unconditional love and faithfulness, provision and grace, and so much more. No matter where you are in life or in what circumstance you find yourself, He's made pledges straight from His heart to yours. Read them, memorize them, and know with full confidence that you are loved and cared for with the greatest capacity ever known to humankind.

PROMISES
FROM
God's Heart

A Bible Promise Journal

DaySpring
LIVE YOUR FAITH

Promises from God's Heart for
COURAGE

Immediately Jesus spoke to them.
"Have courage! It is I. Don't be afraid."
MATTHEW 14:27 CSB

Have I not commanded you?
Be strong and courageous.
Do not be frightened,
and do not be dismayed,
for the Lord your God is
with you wherever you go.
JOSHUA 1:9 ESV

But Christ, God's faithful Son, is in complete
charge of God's house. And we Christians are God's
house—He lives in us!—if we keep up
our courage firm to the end, and our joy
and our trust in the Lord.
HEBREWS 3:6 TLB

Promises from God's Heart for
COMFORT

Blessed are those who mourn,
for they shall be comforted.
MATTHEW 5:4 ESV

The Lord is near the brokenhearted;
He saves those crushed in spirit.
PSALM 34:18 CSB

Praise the God and Father of our
Lord Jesus Christ, the Father
of mercies and the God of all comfort.
He comforts us in all our affliction,
so that we may be able to comfort those
who are in any kind of affliction,
through the comfort we ourselves receive
from God. For as the sufferings of Christ
overflow to us, so through Christ our
comfort also overflows.
II CORINTHIANS 1:3-5 CSB

Promises from God's Heart for
PEACE

*The Lord gives His people strength;
the Lord blesses His people with peace.*
PSALM 29:11 CSB

*Don't worry about anything; instead,
pray about everything; tell God your needs,
and don't forget to thank Him for His answers. If
you do this, you will experience God's peace which
is far more wonderful than the human mind can
understand. His peace will keep your thoughts and
your hearts quiet and at rest as you trust in Christ
Jesus.*
PHILIPPIANS 4:6-7 TLB

*Let the peace that comes from Christ rule in your
hearts. For as members of one body you are called
to live in peace. And always be thankful.*
COLOSSIANS 3:15 NLT

Promises from God's Heart for

JOY

You will go out with joy
and be led out in peace.
The mountains and hills will burst
into song before you,
And all the trees in the fields
will clap their hands.
ISAIAH 55:12 NCV

God will yet fill your mouth
with laughter and your lips
with shouts of joy.
JOB 8:21 NCV

Consider it a great joy, my brothers,
whenever you experience various trials,
knowing that the testing of your faith
produces endurance.
JAMES 1:2-3 CSB

Promises from God's Heart for
CLARITY

Trust in the Lord with all your heart, and
do not rely on your own understanding;
in all your ways know Him, and He will
make your paths straight.
PROVERBS 3:5-6 CSB

For God is not a God
of confusion but of peace.
I CORINTHIANS 14:33 NASB

Now if any of you lacks wisdom, he should
ask God—who gives to all generously and
ungrudgingly—and it will be given to him.
JAMES 1:5 CSB

Promises from God's Heart for
COMPASSION

Through the Lord's mercies
we are not consumed,
Because His compassions fail not,
They are new every morning;
Great is Your faithfulness.
"The Lord is my portion," says my soul,
"Therefore I hope in Him!"
The Lord is good to
those who wait for Him,
To the soul who seeks Him.
LAMENTATIONS 3:22-25 NKJV

Lord, don't hold back Your tender mercies
from me. Let Your unfailing love and
faithfulness always protect me.
PSALM 40:11 NLT

What counts is whether we have been
transformed into a new creation. May
God's peace and mercy be upon all who
live by this principle; they are the new
people of God.
GALATIANS 6:15-16 NLT

Promises from God's Heart for
CONTENTMENT

Why are you in despair, O my soul?
Why have you become restless
and disquieted within me?
Hope in God and wait expectantly
for Him, for I shall yet praise Him,
The help of my countenance and my God.
PSALM 42:11 AMP

Always be full of joy in the Lord; I say it
again, rejoice!...Remember that the Lord
is coming soon. Don't worry about anything;
instead, pray about everything; tell God your
needs...If you do this, you will experience
God's peace...His peace will keep your
thoughts and your hearts quiet and
at rest as you trust in Christ Jesus.
PHILIPPIANS 4:4-7 TLB

If your heart is broken, you'll find God
right there; if you're kicked in the gut,
He'll help you catch your breath.
PSALM 34:18 THE MESSAGE

Promises from God's Heart for
NEW LIFE

Therefore, if anyone is in Christ,
he is a new creation. The old has passed
away; behold, the new has come.
II CORINTHIANS 5:17 ESV

To put off your old self, which belongs
to your former manner of life and
is corrupt through deceitful desires,
and to be renewed in the spirit of your
minds, and to put on the new self,
created after the likeness of God in true
righteousness and holiness.
EPHESIANS 4:22-24 ESV

Behold, I am doing a new thing;
now it springs forth, do you not perceive
it? I will make a way in the wilderness
and rivers in the desert.
ISAIAH 43:19 ESV

Promises from God's Heart for
HOPE

Why, my soul, are you so dejected?
Why are you in such turmoil?
Put your hope in God, for I will still
praise Him, my Savior and my God.
PSALM 42:11 CSB

A man who endures trials is blessed,
because when he passes the test
he will receive the crown of life that
God has promised to those who love Him.
JAMES 1:12 CSB

You will succeed if you carefully
follow the statutes and ordinances
the Lord commanded Moses for Israel.
Be strong and courageous.
Don't be afraid or discouraged.
I CHRONICLES 22:13 CSB

Promises from God's Heart for
UNFAILING LOVE

*We have come to know and
to believe the love that God has for us.
God is love, and whoever abides in love
abides in God, and God abides in him.*
I JOHN 4:16 ESV

*I will rejoice in doing them good,
and I will plant them in this land in
faithfulness, with all my heart
and all my soul.*
JEREMIAH 32:41 ESV

We love Him, because He first loved us.
I JOHN 4:19 NKJV

Promises from God's Heart for
CONFIDENCE

But when he [Peter] saw the strength of the wind, he was afraid, and beginning to sink he cried out, "Lord, save me!" Immediately Jesus reached out His hand, caught hold of him, and said to him, "You of little faith, why did you doubt?" When they got into the boat, the wind ceased.
MATTHEW 14:30-32 CSB

Truly, I say to you, whoever says to this mountain, 'Be taken up and thrown into the sea,' and does not doubt in his heart, but believes that what he says will come to pass, it will be done for him.
MARK 11:23 ESV

Jesus answered them, "Truly I tell you, if you have faith and do not doubt, you will not only do what was done to the fig tree, but even if you tell this mountain, 'Be lifted up and thrown into the sea,' it will be done. And if you believe, you will receive whatever you ask for in prayer."
MATTHEW 21:21-22 CSB

Promises from God's Heart for

REST

*Come to me, all who labor and are heavy
laden, and I will give you rest.*
MATTHEW 11:28 ESV

*Lord, You have been our dwelling
place in all generations...Even from
everlasting to everlasting,
You are God.*
PSALM 90:1-2 NASB

*As for me, I trust in You, O Lord,
I say, "You are my God,"
My times are in Your hand.*
PSALM 31:14-15 NASB

Promises from God's Heart for

ENCOURAGEMENT

Do not fear, for I am with you;
do not be afraid, for I am your God.
I will strengthen you; I will help you;
I will hold on to you with
My righteous right hand.

ISAIAH 41:10 CSB

God, hear my cry; pay attention to
my prayer. I call to You from the ends of
the earth when my heart is without strength.
Lead me to a rock that is high above me,
for You have been a refuge for me,
a strong tower in the face of the enemy.

PSALM 61:1-3 CSB

For I am sure that neither death nor life,
nor angels nor rulers, nor things present
nor things to come, nor powers, nor height
nor depth, nor anything else in all creation,
will be able to separate us from the love of God
in Christ Jesus our Lord.

ROMANS 8:38-39 ESV

Promises from God's Heart for
FAITHFULNESS

Remember Your promise to me,
it is my only hope,
Your promise revives me;
it comforts me in all my troubles....
I meditate on Your age-old regulations;
O Lord, they comfort me....
Your eternal word,
O Lord, Stands firm in heaven.
Your faithfulness extends to every
generation, As enduring as the earth You
created. Your regulations remain
true to this day.
PSALM 119:49-50, 52, 89-91 NLT

Never let loyalty and faithfulness
leave you. Tie them around your neck;
write them on the tablet of your heart.
PROVERBS 3:3 CSB

Promises from God's Heart for
ENDURANCE

I call to God; God will help me.
At dusk, dawn, and noon I sigh
deep sighs — He hears, He rescues.
My life is well and whole, secure....
PSALM 55:16-17 THE MESSAGE

So we must not get tired of doing
good, for we will reap at the
proper time if we don't give up.
GALATIANS 6:9 CSB

The Lord is my fort where I can enter and be safe;
no one can follow me in and slay me. He is a
rugged mountain where I hide; He is my Savior,
a rock where none can reach me, and a tower of
safety. He is my shield. He is like the strong horn
of a mighty fighting bull.
PSALM 18:2 TLB

Promises from God's Heart for
HIS GRACE

*Therefore the Lord is waiting to show
you mercy, and is rising up to show you
compassion, for the Lord is a just God.
All who wait patiently for Him are happy.*
ISAIAH 30:18 CSB

*Lord, be gracious to us! We wait for You.
Be our strength every morning
and our salvation in time of trouble.*
ISAIAH 33:2 CSB

*I believe that I shall look upon
the goodness of the Lord
in the land of the living!*
PSALM 27:13 ESV

ETERNAL LIFE

For God loved the world in this way:
He gave His One and Only Son,
so that everyone who believes in Him
will not perish but have eternal life.

JOHN 3:16 CSB

I tell you the truth, whoever hears what I say
and believes in the One who sent Me has eternal
life. That person will not be judged guilty but
has already left death and entered life.

JOHN 5:24 NCV

For we know that if our earthly tent we live in is
destroyed, we have a building from God, an eternal
dwelling in the heavens, not made with hands.

II CORINTHIANS 5:1 CSB

Promises from God's Heart for
PROTECTION

But now, God's Message,
the God who made you in the first
place,
Jacob, the One who got you started,
Israel: "Don't be afraid, I've redeemed
you.
I've called your name. You're Mine.
When you're in over your head,
I'll be there with you.
When you're in rough waters,
you will not go down.
When you're between a rock
and a hard place, it won't be a dead end—
Because I am God, your personal God,
The Holy of Israel, your Savior.
I paid a huge price for you:
all of Egypt, with rich Cush and Seba
thrown in! That's how much you mean
to Me! That's how much I love you!
ISAIAH 43:1-4 THE MESSAGE

If God is for us, who can be against us?
ROMANS 8:31 ESV

Promises from God's Heart for

HIS FAVOR

For You, Lord, bless the righteous one;
You surround him with favor like a shield.
PSALM 5:12 CSB

How blessed is God! And what a blessing He is!
He's the Father of our Master, Jesus Christ, and
takes us to the high places of blessing in Him.
Long before He laid down earth's foundations, He
had us in mind, had settled on us as the focus of
His love, to be made whole and holy by His love.
EPHESIANS 1:5-6 THE MESSAGE

Blessings on all who reverence and trust the
Lord—on all who obey Him! Their reward shall be
prosperity and happiness.... That is God's reward
to those who reverence and trust Him.
PSALM 128:1-2, 4 TLB

Promises from God's Heart for
HIS CARE

The Lord is my shepherd;
I shall not want.
He makes me to lie down
in green pastures;
He leads me beside the still waters.
He restores my soul;
He leads me in the
paths of righteousness
For His name's sake.

Yea, though I walk through
the valley of the shadow of death,
I will fear no evil; For You are with me;
Your rod and Your staff, they comfort me.

You prepare a table before me
in the presence of my enemies;
You anoint my head with oil;
My cup runs over.
Surely goodness and mercy shall follow
me All the days of my life; And I will
dwell in the house of the Lord Forever.
PSALM 23:1-6 NKJV

HIS FRIENDSHIP

*Friendship with God is reserved
for those who reverence Him.
With them alone He shares the
secrets of His promises.*
PSALM 25:14 TLB

*He guarantees right up to the end that you will
be counted free from all sin and guilt on that
day when He returns. God will surely do this for
you, for He always does just what He says, and He
is the one who invited you into this wonderful
friendship with His Son, even Christ our Lord.*
I CORINTHIANS 1:8-9 TLB

*When I think of You as I lie on my bed,
I meditate on You during the night watches
because You are my helper; I will rejoice
in the shadow of Your wings. I follow close
to You; Your right hand holds on to me.*
PSALM 63:6-8 CSB

Promises from God's Heart for

HIS PURPOSE FOR YOU

Call to Me, and I will answer you,
and show you great and mighty things,
which you do not know.
JEREMIAH 33:3 NKJV

Your ears shall hear a word behind you,
saying, "This is the way, walk in it,"
Whenever you turn to the right hand
Or whenever you turn to the left.
ISAIAH 30:21 NKJV

And we know that all things
work together for good to those
who love God, to those who
are the called according to His purpose.
ROMANS 8:28 NKJV

Promises from God's Heart for

HIS GUIDANCE

*When the Spirit of truth comes, He will
guide you into all the truth. For He will
not speak on His own, but He will speak
whatever He hears. He will also declare
to you what is to come.*
JOHN 16:13 CSB

*Trust in the Lord with all your heart, and do not
rely on your own understanding; in all your ways
know Him, and He will make your paths straight.*
PROVERBS 3:5-6 CSB

*And I will lead the blind in a way
that they do not know, in paths that they
have not known I will guide them. I will
turn the darkness before them into light,
the rough places into level ground. These are
the things I do, and I do not forsake them.*
ISAIAH 42:16 ESV

Promises from God's Heart for
STRENGTH

I ask Him to strengthen you by His Spirit—not a brute strength but a glorious inner strength—that Christ will live in you as you open the door and invite Him in. And I ask Him that with both feet planted firmly on love, you'll be able to take in with all followers of Jesus the extravagant dimensions of Christ's love. Reach out and experience the breadth! Test its length! Plumb the depths! Rise to the heights! Live full lives, full in the fullness of God.

God can do anything, you know—far more than you could ever imagine or guess or request in your wildest dreams! He does it not by pushing us around but by working within us, His Spirit deeply and gently within us.

EPHESIANS 3:16-21 THE MESSAGE

Promises from God's Heart for

HEALING

Do not be wise in your own eyes;
Fear the Lord and turn away from evil.
It will be healing to your body
And refreshment to your bones.

PROVERBS 3:7-8 NASB

Those who trust in the Lord
will renew their strength;
they will soar on wings like eagles;
they will run and not become weary;
they will walk and not faint.

ISAIAH 40:31 CSB

My roots will have access to water,
and the dew will rest on my branches all night.
My whole being will be refreshed within me,
and my bow will be renewed in my hand.

JOB 29:19-20 CSB

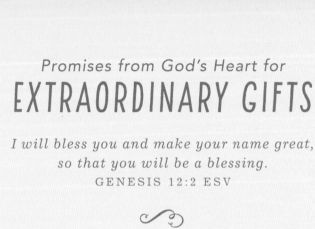

Promises from God's Heart for

EXTRAORDINARY GIFTS

*I will bless you and make your name great,
so that you will be a blessing.*
GENESIS 12:2 ESV

*For we are His workmanship,
created in Christ Jesus for good works,
which God prepared ahead of time
for us to do.*
EPHESIANS 2:10 CSB

*Let all the skilled artisans among you
come and make everything
that the Lord has commanded.*
EXODUS 35:10-11 CSB

Promises from God's Heart for

THE HOPE OF HEAVEN

For we know that if our earthly tent
we live in is destroyed, we have a building
from God, an eternal dwelling in the
heavens, not made with hands.
II CORINTHIANS 5:1 CSB

Whoever does and teaches these commands
will be called great in the kingdom of heaven.
MATTHEW 5:19 CSB

Our citizenship is in heaven, and we
eagerly wait for a Savior from there,
the Lord Jesus Christ. He will transform
the body of our humble condition into the
likeness of His glorious body, by the power
that enables Him to subject
everything to Himself.
PHILIPPIANS 3:20-21 CSB

Promises from God's Heart for
HAPPINESS

*Delight yourself in the LORD,
and he will give you
the desires of your heart.*
PSALM 37:4 ESV

*With joy you will drink deeply
from the fountain of salvation!*
ISAIAH 12:3 NLT

*How happy your people must be!
What a privilege for your officials
to stand here day after day,
listening to your wisdom!*
II CHRONICLES 9:7 NLT

Promises from God's Heart for

HIS MERCY

The Lord is compassionate and merciful.
JAMES 5:11 CSB

*But as for me, I will sing each morning
about Your power and mercy. For You
have been my high tower of refuge, a
place of safety in the day of my distress.*
PSALM 59:16 TLB

*For we do not have a high priest who is unable
to sympathize with our weaknesses, but one who
in every respect has been tempted as we are, yet
without sin. Let us then with confidence draw near
to the throne of grace, that we may receive mercy
and find grace to help in time of need.*
HEBREWS 4:15-16 ESV

Promises from God's Heart for

HIS GOODNESS

*Love and truth belong to God's people;
goodness and peace will be theirs.
On earth people will be loyal to God,
and God's goodness will shine down
from heaven. The Lord will give
His goodness, and the land will give
its crops. Goodness will go before God
and prepare the way for Him.*
PSALM 85:10-13 NCV

*I lavish my love upon thousands of those
who love Me and obey My commandments.*
EXODUS 20:6 TLB

*Say thank You to the Lord
for being so good,
for always being so loving and kind.*
PSALM 107:1 TLB

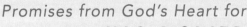

Promises from God's Heart for
HIS POWER

*You will receive power when
the Holy Spirit has come on you.*
ACTS 1:8 CSB

*Ascribe power to God. His majesty is
over Israel, His power among the clouds.
God, You are awe-inspiring in Your
sanctuaries. The God of Israel gives
power and strength to His people.
May God be praised!*
PSALM 68:34-35 CSB

*His divine power has given us
everything required for life
and godliness through the
knowledge of Him who called us
by His own glory and goodness.*
II PETER 1:3 CSB

Promises from God's Heart for
SAFETY

*God is our refuge and strength, a helper
who is always found in times of trouble.
Therefore we will not be afraid.*
PSALM 46:1-2 CSB

*We have this hope as an anchor
for the soul, firm and secure.*
HEBREWS 6:19 CSB

*For you have been a stronghold for the
poor person, a stronghold for the needy
in his distress, a refuge from storms
and a shade from heat.*
ISAIAH 25:4 CSB

Promises from God's Heart for

SERENITY

You keep him in perfect peace
whose mind is stayed on you,
because he trusts in you.
ISAIAH 26:3 ESV

And the peace of God, which surpasses
all understanding, will guard your hearts
and your minds in Christ Jesus.
PHILIPPIANS 4:7 ESV

In the same way the Spirit also helps
us in our weakness, because we do not
know what to pray for as we should,
but the Spirit Himself intercedes for us
with unspoken groanings.
ROMANS 8:26 CSB

Promises from God's Heart for
PATIENCE

*The Lord is not slow to fulfill his
promise as some count slowness, but is
patient toward you, not wishing that any
should perish, but that all should reach
repentance.*
II PETER 3:9 ESV

*But I received mercy for this reason,
that in me, as the foremost, Jesus Christ
might display his perfect patience as an
example to those who were to believe
in him for eternal life.*
I TIMOTHY 1:16 ESV

*Love is patient, love is kind.
Love does not envy,
is not boastful, is not arrogant.*
I CORINTHIANS 13:4 CSB

Promises from God's Heart for a

WORRY-FREE LIFE

*Don't worry about anything, but in
everything, through prayer and petition
with thanksgiving, present your requests
to God. And the peace of God, which
surpasses all understanding, will guard
your hearts and minds in Christ Jesus.*
PHILIPPIANS 4:6 CSB

*And if God provides clothing for the flowers that
are here today and gone tomorrow, don't you
suppose that He will provide clothing for you,
you doubters? And don't worry about food—what to
eat and drink; don't worry at all that God
will provide it for you. All mankind scratches
for its daily bread, but your heavenly Father
knows your needs.*
LUKE 12:28-30 TLB

*Remember, your Father knows exactly
what you need even before you ask Him!*
MATTHEW 6:8 TLB

FORGIVENESS

In Him we have redemption, the
forgiveness of sins.
COLOSSIANS 1:14 CSB

Do not judge, and you will not be judged.
Do not condemn, and you
will not be condemned.
Forgive, and you will be forgiven.
LUKE 6:37 CSB

Blessed and happy
and favored are those whose
lawless acts have been forgiven,
and whose sins have been
covered up and completely buried.
ROMANS 4:7 AMP

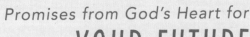

Promises from God's Heart for
YOUR FUTURE

*For I know the plans I have for you,
declares the Lord, plans for welfare
and not for evil, to give you a
future and a hope.*
JEREMIAH 29:11 ESV

*Keep your voice from weeping and your eyes
from tears, for the reward for your work
will come—this is the Lord's declaration...
There is hope for your future—
This is the Lord's declaration.*
JEREMIAH 31:16-17 CSB

*Honey whets the appetite and so does wisdom!
When you enjoy becoming wise, there is
hope for you! A bright future lies ahead!*
PROVERBS 24:14 TLB

Promises from God's Heart in
TIMES OF GRIEF

*The Lord is close to
the brokenhearted, and He saves
those whose spirits have been crushed.*
PSALM 34:18 NCV

*What a wonderful God we have—
He is the Father of our Lord Jesus Christ,
the source of every mercy, and the one
who so wonderfully comforts and
strengthens us in our hardships and trials.
And why does He do this? So that when
others are troubled, needing our sympathy
and encouragement, we can pass on to
them this same help and comfort
God has given us.*
II CORINTHIANS 1:3-4 TLB

*But I will send you the Comforter—
the Holy Spirit, the source of all truth.
He will come to you from the Father
and will tell you all about Me.*
JOHN 15:26 TLB

Promises from God's Heart for
HIS RETURN

*But I tell you, in the future you will
see the Son of Man seated at the
right hand of the Power and coming
on the clouds of heaven.*
MATTHEW 26:64 CSB

*Now concerning how and when all this will
happen, dear brothers and sisters, we don't
really need to write you. For you know quite
well that the day of the Lord's return will come
unexpectedly, like a thief in the night.*
I THESSALONIANS 5:1-2 NLT

*For the Son of Man is going to come
with His angels in the glory of His
Father, and then He will reward each
according to what he has done.*
MATTHEW 16:27 CSB

THE HOLY SPIRIT

*And I will ask the Father,
and He will give you
another Counselor to be with
you forever. He is the Spirit of truth.
The world is unable to receive Him
because it doesn't see Him or
know Him. But you do know Him,
because He remains with you
and will be in you.*

JOHN 14:16-18 CSB

*John [the Baptist] answered them
all, "I baptize you with water,
but One is coming who is more
powerful than I…. He will baptize
you with the Holy Spirit."*

LUKE 3:16 CSB

*I will give you a new heart
and put a new spirit within you;
I will remove your heart of stone and
give you a heart of flesh. I will place My
Spirit within you and cause you to follow
My statutes and carefully observe
My ordinances.*

EZEKIEL 36:26-27 CSB

Promises from God's Heart for

WISDOM

I will bless the Lord who counsels me—
Even at night when my thoughts trouble me....
Because He is at my right hand.
I will not be shaken.
PSALM 16:7-8 CSB

Let a wise person listen and increase learning,
and let a discerning person obtain guidance.
PROVERBS 1:5 CSB

For whatever was written in the past was
written for our instruction, so that we may
have hope through endurance and through
the encouragement from the Scriptures.
ROMANS 15:4 CSB

Promises from God's Heart for
RENEWAL

*He will wipe away every tear from
their eyes, and death shall be no more,
neither shall there be mourning,
nor crying, nor pain anymore,
for the former things have passed away.*
REVELATION 21:4 ESV

*He saved us, not because of works done by
us in righteousness, but according to his
own mercy, by the washing of regeneration
and renewal of the Holy Spirit.*
TITUS 3:5 ESV

*Create in me a clean heart, O God,
and renew a right spirit within me.*
PSALM 51:10 ESV

Promises from God's Heart for
FREEDOM

*Now the Lord is the Spirit;
and where the Spirit of the Lord is,
there is freedom.*
II CORINTHIANS 3:17 CSB

*My brothers and sisters,
God called you to be free,
but do not use your freedom
as an excuse to do what
pleases your sinful self.
Serve each other with love.*
GALATIANS 5:13 NCV

*I will walk freely in an open place
because I seek Your precepts.*
PSALM 119:45 CSB

Promises from God's Heart for a
STRONG FOUNDATION

*Everyone then who hears these words
of mine and does them will be like a wise
man who built his house on the rock.
And the rain fell, and the floods came,
and the winds blew and beat on that
house, but it did not fall, because it had
been founded on the rock.*
MATTHEW 7:24-25 ESV

*For no one can lay a foundation
other than that which is laid,
which is Jesus Christ.*
I CORINTHIANS 3:11 ESV

*I can do everything God asks me
to with the help of Christ
who gives me the strength and power.*
PHILIPPIANS 4:13 TLB

Promises from God's Heart

WHEN YOU PRAY

*Call to Me and I will answer you
and tell you great and incomprehensible
things you do not know.*
JEREMIAH 33:3 CSB

*But when you pray, go into your most private
room, close the door and pray to your Father
who is in secret, and your Father who sees
[what is done] in secret will reward you.*
MATTHEW 6:6 AMP

*Ask, and it will be given to you.
Seek, and you will find. Knock, and the door
will be opened to you. For everyone who asks
receives, and the one who seeks finds,
and to the one who knocks,
the door will be opened.*
MATTHEW 7:7-8 CSB

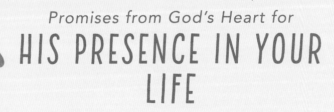

Promises from God's Heart for

HIS PRESENCE IN YOUR LIFE

The Lord is in His holy temple;
the Lord—His throne is in heaven.
His eyes watch; His gaze
examines everyone.
PSALM 11:4 CSB

Draw near to God, and
He will draw near to you.
JAMES 4:8 CSB

But let all who take refuge in You rejoice;
let them shout for joy forever ....
For You, Lord, bless the righteous one;
You surround him with favor like a shield.
PSALM 5:11-12 CSB

Promises from God's Heart for

HIS PROVISION

Young lions lack food and go hungry,
but those who seek the Lord will not
lack any good thing.
PSALM 34:10 CSB

Bring the full tithe into the storehouse, that there
may be food in my house. And thereby put me to
the test, says the Lord of hosts, if I will not open
the windows of heaven for you and pour down
for you a blessing until there is no more need.
MALACHI 3:10 ESV

He waters the mountains from His palace...
He causes grass to grow for the livestock
and provides crops for man to cultivate,
producing food from the earth...and
bread that sustains human hearts.
PSALM 104:13-15 CSB

Promises from God's Heart for

WHEN YOU STRAY

If a man has a hundred sheep,
and one wanders away and is lost,
what will he do? Won't he leave the
ninety-nine others and go out into
the hills to search for the lost one?
And if he finds it, he will rejoice over it
more than over the ninety-nine others
safe at home!
MATTHEW 18:12-13 TLB

Or what woman who has ten silver coins,
if she loses one coin, does not light
a lamp, sweep the house, and search
carefully until she finds it? When she finds
it, she calls her friends and neighbors
together, saying, 'Rejoice with me, because
I have found the silver coin I lost!"'
LUKE 15:8-9 CSB

The one who conceals his sins will not
prosper, but whoever confesses and
renounces them will find mercy.
PROVERBS 28:13 CSB

WHEN YOU ARE WEAK AND WEARY

*Come to Me, all of you who are weary
and burdened, and I will give you rest.
Take up My yoke and learn from Me,
because I am lowly and humble in heart,
and you will find rest for your souls.*
MATTHEW 11:28-29 CSB

*Remember Your word to Your servant;
You have given me hope through it.
This is my comfort in my affliction:
Your promise has given me life.*
PSALM 119:49-50 CSB

*"My grace is sufficient for you,
for power is perfected in weakness."
Therefore, I [Paul] will most gladly
boast all the more about my weaknesses,
so that Christ's power may reside in me.*
II CORINTHIANS 12:9 CSB

Promises from God's Heart for
HIS VICTORY

*Now I know that the Lord gives victory to
His anointed; He will answer him
from His holy heaven with mighty
victories from His right hand.*
PSALM 20:6 CSB

*A horse is prepared for the
day of battle, but victory
comes from the Lord.*
PROVERBS 21:31 CSB

*The Lord is on my side; I will not fear.
What can man do to me?
The Lord is on my side as my helper;
I shall look in triumph on
those who hate me.*
PSALM 118:6-7 ESV

Promises from God's Heart for

HIS TRUTH

*You will know the truth, and
the truth will set you free.*
JOHN 8:32 CSB

*The sum of your word is truth,
and every one of your righteous
rules endures forever.*
PSALM 119:160 ESV

*When you heard the message of truth,
the gospel of your salvation, and when you
believed in Him, you were also sealed with
the promised Holy Spirit. He is the
down payment of our inheritance,
for the redemption of the possession,
to the praise of His glory.*
EPHESIANS 1:13-14 CSB

Promises from God's Heart for
KINDNESS

But when the time came for the kindness and love of God our Savior to appear, then He saved us—not because we were good enough to be saved but because of His kindness and pity—by washing away our sins and giving us the new joy of the indwelling Holy Spirit, whom He poured out upon us with wonderful fullness—and all because of what Jesus Christ our Savior did so that He could declare us good in God's eyes—all because of His great kindness; and now we can share in the wealth of the eternal life He gives us, and we are eagerly looking forward to receiving it.
TITUS 3:4-7 TLB

Show me the kindness of the Lord as long as I live.
I SAMUEL 20:14 NCV

Promises from God's Heart

WHEN YOU NEED RESCUE

Give justice to the weak and the fatherless; maintain the right of the afflicted and the destitute. Rescue the weak and the needy; deliver them from the hand of the wicked.

PSALM 82:3-4 ESV

The salvation of the righteous is from the Lord; he is their stronghold in the time of trouble.

PSALM 37:39 ESV

Then they cried to the Lord in their trouble, and He brought them out of their distress.

PSALM 107:28 CSB

Promises from God's Heart for
FULLNESS

Christ may dwell in your hearts through faith—that you, being rooted and grounded in love, may have strength to comprehend with all the saints what is the breadth and length and height and depth, and to know the love of Christ that surpasses knowledge, that you may be filled with all the fullness of God.
EPHESIANS 3:17-19 ESV

Everything of God gets expressed in Him, so you can see and hear Him clearly. You don't need a telescope, a microscope, or a horoscope to realize the fullness of Christ, and the emptiness of the universe without Him. When you come to Him, that fullness comes together for you, too. His power extends over everything.
COLOSSIANS 2:9-10 THE MESSAGE

Promises from God's Heart for
ACCEPTANCE

Because, if you confess with your mouth that Jesus is Lord and believe in your heart that God raised him from the dead, you will be saved. For with the heart one believes and is justified, and with the mouth one confesses and is saved. For the Scripture says, "Everyone who believes in him will not be put to shame." For there is no distinction between Jew and Greek; for the same Lord is Lord of all, bestowing his riches on all who call on him. For "everyone who calls on the name of the Lord will be saved."

ROMANS 10:9-13 ESV

For God so loved the world, that he gave his only Son, that whoever believes in him should not perish but have eternal life.

JOHN 3:16 ESV

The One who died for us—who was raised to life for us!—is in the presence of God at this very moment sticking up for us. Do you think anyone is going to be able to drive a wedge between us and Christ's love for us? There is no way!

ROMANS 8:31-39 THE MESSAGE

Promises from God's Heart for
RELEASE

*Humble yourselves before the Lord,
and He will exalt you.*
JAMES 4:10 CSB

*But seek first the kingdom of God and His
righteousness, and all these things will
be provided for you.*
MATTHEW 6:33 CSB

*Be still, and know that I am God. I will
be exalted among the nations, I will be
exalted in the earth!*
PSALM 46:10 ESV

Promises from God's Heart for

HARD TIMES

*Be strong and courageous; don't be terrified
or afraid of them. For the Lord your God is
the one who will go with you;
He will not leave you or abandon you.*
DEUTERONOMY 31:6 CSB

*Therefore we do not give up; even though
our outer person is being destroyed, our inner
person is being renewed day by day.*
II CORINTHIANS 4:16 CSB

*Keep your eyes on Jesus, our leader and instructor.
He was willing to die a shameful death on the
cross because of the joy He knew would be His
afterwards; and now He sits in the place of honor
by the throne of God.*
HEBREWS 12:2 TLB

Promises from God's Heart regarding

BEING HELD

Do not fear, for I am with you;
do not be afraid, for I am your God.
I will strengthen you; I will help you;
I will hold on to you with
My righteous right hand.
ISAIAH 41:10 CSB

Behold, I have engraved you on
the palms of my hands; your walls
are continually before me.
ISAIAH 49:16 ESV

Even there Your hand will guide me,
Your strength will support me.
PSALM 139:10 TLB

Promises from God's Heart: A Bible Promise Journal
© 2019 DaySpring Cards, Inc. All rights reserved.
First Edition, August 2019
Published by:

P.O. Box 1010
Siloam Springs, AR 72761
dayspring.com

Printed in China
Prime: J1481
ISBN: 978-1-64454-431-0